Weird SPORTS

by Michael Teitelbaum

Beach Ball Books

Beach Ball Books

Published by Beach Ball Books LLC
www.beachballbooks.com

Produced by Shoreline Publishing Group LLC
Santa Barbara, California
www.shorelinepublishing.com
President/Editorial Director: James Buckley, Jr.
Designed by Tom Carling, www.carlingdesign.com
Cover design by John Roshell of Comicraft
Cover illustrations by Steve Buccellato

Text copyright © 2011 by Michael Teitelbaum
Photo credits on page 48.

ISBN: 978-1-936310-03-6 (paperback)
ISBN: 978-1-936310-14-2 (hardcover)

10 9 8 7 6 5 4 3 2   09 10 11 12 13

This book conforms to CPSIA 2008.

Printed by in Canada. October, 2011.

CONTENTS

SPECIAL SECTION I: WEIRD WORLD OF SPORTS

WELCOME TO THE WEIRDNESS!

Caber tossing, page 26

Welcome to the Weird World of Sports. You did bring your snorkel, your toilet, and your frozen turkey, didn't you? Good. Because all of these things are used in the oddball sports in this book.

What do we mean by "weird"? Good question.

A whole world of competitions takes place outside of the major team and individual sports that everybody knows about (you know: basketball, soccer, football, etc.). For most of these offbeat sports, you don't have to be a world-class athlete in top shape to play. You just have to be brave and (sometimes) not afraid of a little pain and suffering.

Being a little bit goofy doesn't hurt, either.

Why do people take part in weird sports like chasing cheese down a hill, tossing a telephone pole, or playing hockey underwater? Basically, the answer is . . . why not? Some of these unusual sports—caber tossing, camel racing, and the Eskimo high kick, for example—have been played for centuries and are part of traditional cultures. Others, such as turkey bowling and speed golf, are versions of more well-known sports. Still others are, well . . . just weird! And here we're talking about mullet-tossing, extreme unicycling, and wife-carrying, among others.

Weird also means different things in different parts of the world. People in some countries think baseball is pretty weird, for

Elephant soccer, page 34

instance. We've tried to pick sports that would be considered a bit different by most people, but we know that in some cases millions of fans cheer for their heroes in these sports, such as sepak takraw and kabaddi.

So what is weird? We think that, in some way, all the sports here are a bit weird. But they're also fun for the people who play them . . . and fun for people to watch. Maybe they'll inspire you to create your own weird sport! Now strap on your lawnmower racing helmet, climb on your soccer-playing elephant, heat up your iron, and jump on the walrus skin* . . . it's time to play some weird sports!

*Don't worry: We'll explain why you need all those things.

Don't Say We Didn't Warn You!

We have to write this because we're grownups: The sports in this book are for reading about only. PLEASE do not try them yourselves at home or at school. When you're an adult, feel free to try them all (and even then be careful) and then let us know how it goes. But until then, these sports are not for kids to try without lots of adult supervision. Okay . . . on with the show!

BOG SNORKELING

What's cold, wet, muddy, thick, and filthy? No, not a really gross dirt milkshake . . . it's a bog. Bogs are very wet, mushy, smelly ground. And believe it or not, people snorkel in them. Yuck! Here's how bog snorkeling works. Swimmers paddle through a narrow trench 60 yards (55 m) long filled with water. The trench is cut from a thick peat bog in Wales (a part of Britain). Only the swimmers' snorkels may remain above the water.

Bog snorkeling has been compared to swimming through pea soup—just not as tasty! The record, set at the 2010 World Championships, is held by Peter Cunningham of Dublin, Ireland, with a time of 1 minute, 24 seconds.

Mountain Bikes, Too!

Don't feel like swimming while you bog snorkel—and really, who can blame you? Then try the mountain-bike version. Mountain-bike bog riders use a special (weighted) bike to squelch along the bottom of the bog, while wearing their snorkels. Bike helmets are not required. Good lungs are.

THE RULES (There Are Rules?)

Bog snorkelers must swim two consecutive lengths of a 60-yard (55 m) water-filled trench cut through a peat bog. The fastest time wins. Competitors must complete the course without using regular swimming strokes, such as the breast stroke. They must rely on flipper power alone.

GEAR UP!

* scuba diving mask
* snorkel
* flippers
* wet suit

UNDERWATER HOCKEY

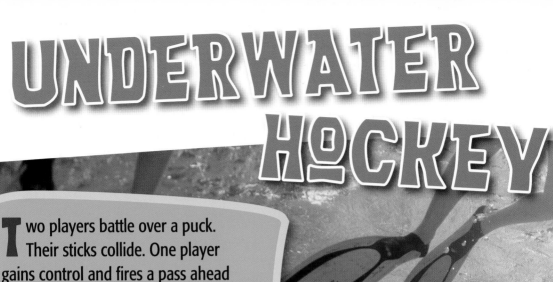

Two players battle over a puck. Their sticks collide. One player gains control and fires a pass ahead to a teammate. The teammate shoots the puck toward the goal—and scores! And now it's time to go up for some air. Some air?

That's right. Welcome to the world of underwater hockey, also called Octopush. In this non-contact sport, two teams compete to move a puck across the bottom of a swimming pool using small sticks, and then shoot the puck into the other team's goal. Same as ice hockey—only the water isn't frozen!

GEAR UP!

* **scuba diving mask** (swimming goggles are not recommended)
* **snorkel** (for breathing)
* **swimming cap** (water polo caps are the preferred choice and they also help protect the ears)
* **flippers** (swim like the fishes)
* **swimsuit** (duh!)
* **glove** (usually a heavy-duty gardening glove, worn on the stick-holding hand)
* **curved wooden or plastic stick** (about 12 inches [30 cm] long)
* **puck** (about the size of an ice hockey puck, but made of plastic-covered lead)

PRO TIP

"You can go down and hold your breath for two or two and half minutes so you can make a great play, but when you come up for air you're going to be dead. So you have to find that balance of making a great play, but also keeping up your energy for the next one that's going to happen right away."

—JORDAN FRYERS, CALGARY UNDERWATER HOCKEY CLUB

THE RULES (There Are Rules?)

Two teams of 10 players each compete, with six players per team in action at any given time. Four subs (no, not submarines) sit on the bench—actually, on the side of the pool or in the water at the surface. The rules are similar to ice hockey, except no body contact (like checking) is allowed unless your stick is on the puck. The puck is passed and shot, just like in ice hockey. Games include two 15-minute halves.

MULLET TOSSING

What could be simpler? You grab a mullet (from a bucket, not from the ocean) and see how far you can throw it. That's it. A mullet, by the way, is a type of fish native to the southern United States.

Fishy trivia time! A mullet is the only fish with a gizzard, a special stomach with muscles strong enough to grind up food. The fish is also said to possess mystical powers. But there's nothing mystical about mullet tossing. Mullet tossing is fun for the tossers and not as much fun for the mullets.

THE RULES
(There Are Rules?)

A player stands at a line in the sand and throws the mullet as far as possible. The longest toss wins. Players generally use one of two tossing techniques. Some grab the fish by the tail and heave it with an underhand toss, like a softball pitcher. Others fold the fish in half or roll it into a ball (a messy affair, to be sure) and throw it overhand, like a quarterback trying to complete a forward pass.

The most famous mullet-tossing tournament is the Flora-Bama Interstate Mullet Toss. It's held each April on the beach, right at the Florida-Alabama border. The object there is for a player standing in one state to toss his or her mullet across the state line into the other state.

Other Flying Fish

Tuna Throwing: At Tunarama in Australia, people throw tuna. A short rope is tied to a very large fish. The throwers spin around and then let fly . . . the world record is 115 feet (35 m)! They've been doing this every year since 1961. Starting in 2008, however, they switched from wasting good fish to using wooden tuna replicas.

Fish Market Flinging: Seattle's famous Pike Place (right) Market sells fish fresh fish from around the world. When a customer buys a particularly large fish, the workers fling the fish from counter to wrapper. You have to keep your eyes open when you're walking the aisles of the market . . . fish are flying!

PRO TIP

"Most people take the fish and roll it up like a baseball, tight as they can, crunch its little bones and everything else. After you throw you have to retrieve your fish. And if it's not too messed up, you wash it off and throw it back in the bucket so another competitor can use it."

—BARBARA BURNS, HOSTESS OF THE ANNUAL FLORA-BAMA TOURNAMENT

WATERFALL KAYAKING

Other than a pretty good way to break your neck, waterfall kayaking is exactly what it sounds like. A person in a kayak paddles toward the edge of a waterfall and then . . . continues right over the edge. The waterfall kayaker must try to maintain control of the kayak, keeping it in touch with the powerful jets of water plunging downward.

Going over a waterfall and landing in one piece (both kayak and kayaker, that is) is the point of this sport. The longer the drop, the greater the fame. The world record is held by Tyler Bradt, who successfully went over Washington State's Palouse Falls, a 186-foot (57 m) drop.

GEAR UP!
* helmet
* life vest
* kayak
* paddle

PRO TIP

"There was a stillness. Then an acceleration, speed, and impact unlike anything I've ever felt before. When I landed, I wasn't sure if I was hurt or not. My body was just in shock."

–TYLER BRADT,
WORLD RECORD HOLDER

EXTREME UNICYCLING

It's hard enough to ride a unicycle. You need good balance, coordination, and lots of practice. But extreme unicyclists take the sport . . . well, to the extreme. Competitors ride their unicycles off-road on uneven terrain like grass, dirt, rocks, ice, snow, and, most grueling of all, up and down mountains. They also ride on handrails and ledges and hop up onto platforms. And, unlike most bikes, unicycles are direct drive, meaning that you have no gears and are always pedaling, uphill and downhill. It's impossible to coast.

GEAR UP!

* **unicycle** (okay, you figured that one out)
* **bike helmet** (a must)
* **knee and elbow pads**
* **wrist and shin guards**
* **padded cycling shorts**
* **gloves**

The Extreme Unicycling Championships

Unicyclists compete in three categories:
* **Street:** riders ride on rails, building ledges, and other city structures
* **Trial:** riders hop their unicycles onto platforms and other obstacles
* **Flatland:** two riders compete head to head, doing tricks and stunts

Unicycle Hockey

Riding a unicycle up and down mountains not extreme enough for you? How about unicycle hockey? The name says it all. Players ride unicycles while using hockey sticks to pass and shoot a ball into the goal. No skates or ice required.

EXTREME IRONING

Ready, set, iron! Oh wait, first climb a mountain, hike into a forest, paddle out to the middle of a river, ski or snowboard down a snowy slope, balance on top of a large statue, stand in the middle of a busy street, parachute from a plane, ride a bike, dive underwater, or walk out on a tightrope above a deep mountain gorge. Okay, are you out there?

Now you're ready for extreme ironing!

Really—that's it. Extreme ironers set themselves up in a very tricky place . . . and then they iron clothes.

GEAR UP!

* iron
* ironing board
* piece of wrinkled clothing
* whatever gear you need for the sport you're doing
* very long extension cord (optional)

THE RULES
(There Are Rules?)

Extreme ironers can be doing a variety of activities, as long as wherever they are and whatever else they are doing, they are also ironing a piece of clothing.

PRO TIP

"Extreme ironing is the latest danger sport that combines the thrills of an extreme outdoor activity with the satisfaction of a well-pressed shirt."

—EXTREMEIRONING.COM

RACiNG

The racers zoom around the track, pedal to the metal, engines screaming, exhaust fumes blasting. Suddenly, a racer pulls up next to you. You push your lawnmower forward, jockeying for the lead. Wait a sec . . . lawnmower?

The highly competitive world of lawnmower racing is no Sunday, cut-the-grass-and-sip-a-lemonade mower ride. Racers drive souped-up, ride-on lawnmowers around a circular or oval dirt track. The racers use the mowers' original engines, blazing at speeds up to 30 mph (48 kph)! The world record is nearly 100 mph (161 kph)! Fortunately, the cutting blades of the mowers are removed for safety. The sport attracts drivers of all ages. It's popular in Britain and some places in the United States.

Who Thought This Up?

Lawnmower racing got its start in 1973 in a pub in West Sussex, England. A group of friends were complaining about how expensive it was to get involved with traditional motor sports. They quickly realized they each already owned a motor vehicle— one that they foolishly used just to mow grass. Lose the blades, find a track, and bingo! A brand new weird sport was born.

GEAR UP!

* ride-on lawnmower
* motorcycle helmet
* gloves

TOILET RACING

Lawnmower racing not weird enough for you? Okay then, picture this. You're sitting on a toilet—lid down, of course—with all your clothes on. The toilet has a motor and handlebars. You take off down a track, trying to outrace the toilet next to you. That's toilet racing!

Toilet races often take place on tracks formed by large, colorful, blow-up walls that can be arranged in different formations.

THE RULES
(There Are Rules?)

* All racers must have one clean toilet.
* All toilets must be capable of being steered both left and right.
* All toilets must have a brake for stopping.
* The toilet lid must remain closed and the driver must remain clothed.

GEAR UP!

* **toilet**
* **battery-operated motor**
* **handlebars** (for steering)
* **brakes** (for stopping—of course!)
* **helmet** (for emergencies—no, not those kinds of emergencies)

BED RACING

You're stretched out in bed with the covers pulled up tight. Time for sleep? No way! It's time for a race. In the weird sport of bed racing, a bed is placed on wheels. One person lies in the bed while four other people push and pull the bed down the course. Many races are run for charity.

THE RULES (There Are Rules?)

* Runners (the people pushing the bed) must start and stop the bed under their own power.
* Beds may not be pulled with ropes or chains.
* No motors or engines of any kind—human power only!
* One person must be on the bed at all times during the race.
* Beds must have headboards and footboards.
* Beds must be raced either head first or foot first—never sideways.

POLAR

THE RULES
(There Are Rules?)

* The 100-mile racers must complete their race within three days.

* The 300-mile racers must complete their race within 4½ days.

* The 430-mile racers must complete their race within 13 days.

* Racers must carry full camping, lighting, and cooking gear, as well as clothing for all the harsh weather conditions they will most likely encounter.

MARATHONING

You know what a marathon is—a running race that covers a grueling 26.2 miles (42.2 km), often through the streets of a major city. Now take those runners, move them to the North or South Pole, have them run that long distance in frigid, snowy conditions, amid ice floes, snow drifts, and biting wind—and you've got a polar marathon. But that's not all. Some competitors run the standard marathon distance, but others run races of 100, 300, even 430 miles (161, 483, 692 km)!

In addition to the athletes who run, there are also those who cross-country ski, ride mountain bikes, or compete by skijoring (see page 24). It's just another race, except for the extreme conditions.

GEAR UP!

* **insulated boots**
* **lightweight but warm parka**
* **goggles** (preferably shaded for the glare of sun on snow)
* **hiking poles** (optional)
* **insulated face mask**
* **camping and cooking gear**

PRO TIP

"I've been at the North Pole before, but this was pleasantly different. The race is a combination of two things I enjoy: polar challenges and marathon running. It's a great test of fitness and stamina."

—SIR RANULPH FIENNES,
BRITISH POLAR EXPLORER

23

SKIJORING

Don't feel up to running a polar marathon? No problem. Try skijoring. Skijoring is a winter sport in which a person on skis is pulled by a horse, a dog (or dogs), or a motor vehicle. The name is Norwegian: *skijoring* means "ski driving."

GEAR UP!

* skis
* ski poles
* goggles
* gloves
* ropes
* harnesses
* something to pull you

DOG SKIJORING

In dog skijoring, the cross-country skier still propels him or herself forward using skis and poles, but the dog or dogs add additional power by running and pulling. The skier wears a skijoring harness, the dog wears a sled dog harness, and the two are connected by a length of rope.

HORSE SKIJORING

In horse skijoring, usually known as equestrian skijoring, a single horse, generally guided by a rider, pulls a person on skis. The skier carries no poles and simply hangs onto a tow rope in a manner similar to water skiing. In some competitions (especially those in France), the horse is riderless and is guided only by the skier.

H ave you ever thought about throwing a telephone pole? Didn't think so. But at the Scottish Highland Games—traditional Scottish athletic events held at sites around the world—athletes toss a caber (KAY-ber). A caber is a large wooden pole, similar to a telephone pole or an electric power pole. The caber toss, however, is not simply a test of strength. The object is not the distance of the throw, but rather how the pole lands.

THE RULES
(There Are Rules?)

The caber tosser grips the tall pole at the bottom and balances it against his shoulder. Then he takes a running start and flips the caber up and over. The object of the sport is to toss the caber so that it falls directly away from the thrower when it lands. A perfect throw lands with the top end of the pole nearest to the thrower and the bottom end (the end the thrower was holding) pointing directly away. To score the throw, picture the hour hand on a clock. A perfect toss is 12 o'clock, straight up and down.

CABER TOSSING

GEAR UP!

* **caber**
* **sturdy shoes:** the caber would hurt if it fell on your toe!
* **wide leather belt:** good for back support
* **kilt** (optional)
* **underwear** (also optional, as long as you wear the kilt)

Other Stuff to Toss

Tossing large wooden poles doesn't appeal to you? How about tossing a 200-pound (91 kg) rock? The sport of *steintossen*, dating back to Switzerland in the 13th century, is played by lifting a heavy stone over your head and tossing it as far as you can. The best throws have reached more than 10 feet (3 m). Steintossen is an important part of Unspunnenfest, an annual celebration of Swiss culture that also includes wrestling and yodeling competitions.

TURKEY BOWLING

N o, turkey bowling does not involve turkeys rolling little balls down a lane (though that would be really cool!). Turkey bowling is a sport based on regular bowling, with two big differences—the bowlers aim a frozen turkey instead of a bowling ball, and the target is 10 big plastic bottles, not bowling pins. Turkey bowling often accompanies Thanksgiving celebrations. Perhaps the most popular of all poultry-related sports, turkey bowling is often used as a half-time event at minor league hockey games in the United States and Canada.

GEAR UP!

* **frozen turkey** (make sure it's fully frozen—otherwise you'll end up with a drippy, slimy, smelly mess)
* **10 large plastic soda bottles** (empty, please, otherwise you'll end up with a drippy . . . you get the idea)

THE RULES (There Are Rules?)

The turkey bowler slides the frozen turkey down a smooth surface, such as ice or linoleum, trying to knock down as many bottles as possible. Scoring is the same as in non-turkey bowling, with strikes and spares. The most bottles knocked down wins.

Who Thought of This?

The origin of the sport of turkey bowling, certainly one of the great moments in the history of weird sports, is believed to have been when bored shoppers began sliding frozen turkeys down the aisle of a grocery store toward a display of soft drink bottles.

SPEED GOLF

A great golfer like Tiger Woods (right) or Karrie Webb can complete an 18-hole golf course in as few as 60 shots. But can they do it in less than 50 minutes? This is the key question behind speed golf. Speed golf—also known as extreme golf, fitness golf, or hit-and-run golf—involves playing an entire round of golf in the lowest mix of strokes and time. Players <u>run</u> from hole to hole and to reach their ball between shots. You have to be a good golfer, but you also have to be in good shape. Some golf courses can be as long as 7,000 yards. That's about 4 miles (6.5 km)!

And the Winner Is...

The lowest score in competition was shot by Christopher Smith at the Chicago Speed Golf Classic on October 16, 2005. Smith hit 65 shots in just 44:06, for a speed golf world record score of 109:06.

THE RULES
(There Are Rules?)

A player's score is calculated by adding the number of minutes it takes for him or her to finish 18 holes and the number of strokes the golfer took. A round of 90 strokes completed in 50 minutes and 30 seconds would compute to a score of 140:30.

WEiRD ANiMAL

Everyone's heard of horse racing, right? But did you know that people stage races using all kinds of animals? Here are some of the weirdest.

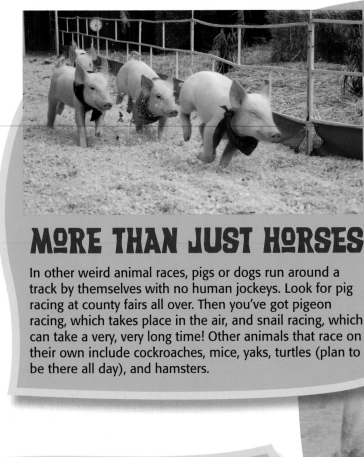

MORE THAN JUST HORSES

In other weird animal races, pigs or dogs run around a track by themselves with no human jockeys. Look for pig racing at county fairs all over. Then you've got pigeon racing, which takes place in the air, and snail racing, which can take a very, very long time! Other animals that race on their own include cockroaches, mice, yaks, turtles (plan to be there all day), and hamsters.

MAN VS. HORSE

One type of horse racing that qualifies as weird is human versus horse cross-country. A human runner competes against a horse (and rider) over a 22-mile (35-km) course. The fastest time for a horse in an annual race in Wales was 1 hour, 30 minutes by a horse named Hussar in 1991. The fastest time for a human was 1 hour, 57 minutes by a man named Paul Wheeler in 1987.

RACES

In some weird animal races, jockeys mount up in saddles, just like in horse racing. In camel races, the jockeys speed around a track, trying to cross the finish line first. In ostrich racing, the world's largest birds are also sometimes ridden using saddles—something that just wouldn't work on your pet parakeet. Sometimes the ostrich pulls a cart in which the driver sits, like trotters in horse racing.

WEIRD WORLD OF SPORTS

Weird is often in the eye (or mind) of the beholder. And it's no different with weird sports. In these next few pages we will look at weird sports from around the world. They might seem weird to you, but many are beloved in their home countries. Such as . . .

ELEPHANT SOCCER

PLAYED IN: **THAILAND AND INDIA**

The soccer player races down the field and reaches for the ball with its trunk. That's right, its trunk! Welcome to the wild world of elephant soccer. In one version, humans ride elephants, playing against other humans riding elephants. The humans don't touch the ball. They just guide the elephants toward the ball and the four-legged giants do the rest—kicking, passing, and shooting. In another version, humans compete against elephants, being careful to avoid having their opponents crush them!

THE RULES
(There Are Rules?)

The rules are pretty much the same as in regular soccer (except for the elephant part). Players can advance the ball with any part of their bodies except their hands—though of course, elephants don't have hands. Some elephant athletes use their trunks, too.

GEAR UP!

* elephants
* elephant drivers (known as "mahouts")
* soccer ball
* 2 goal nets

SEPAK TAKRAW

PLAYED IN: THAILAND, MALAYSIA, AND OTHER PLACES

The ball goes flying back and forth over the net. Players on each team keep the ball in the air, passing or setting up a powerful spike, hoping to send the ball slamming to the court on the other side of the net to score a point. Volleyball? Well, yes, but with a twist. Players can't use their hands! In sepak takraw (SEE-pack TAHK-raw), also known as kick volleyball, players are only allowed to use their feet, knees, chest, and head to touch the ball—kind of a blend of soccer and volleyball.

GEAR UP!

* **plastic ball** about the size of a large softball, made of woven strips. Used to be made of rattan.
* **net** that is 5 feet (1.52 m) high
* **court** measuring 44 by 20 feet (13.4 by 6.1 m)

PRO TIP

"The inside kick is the kick used most often in sepak takraw. The inside kick is used to set up spikes, and it allows you to put the ball in the correct position in the air. To practice it, throw the ball onto your strong foot with your knee bent and parallel to the ground, and pop the ball up in the air."

—SUEBSAK PASUEB, THAILAND
considered best player in the world

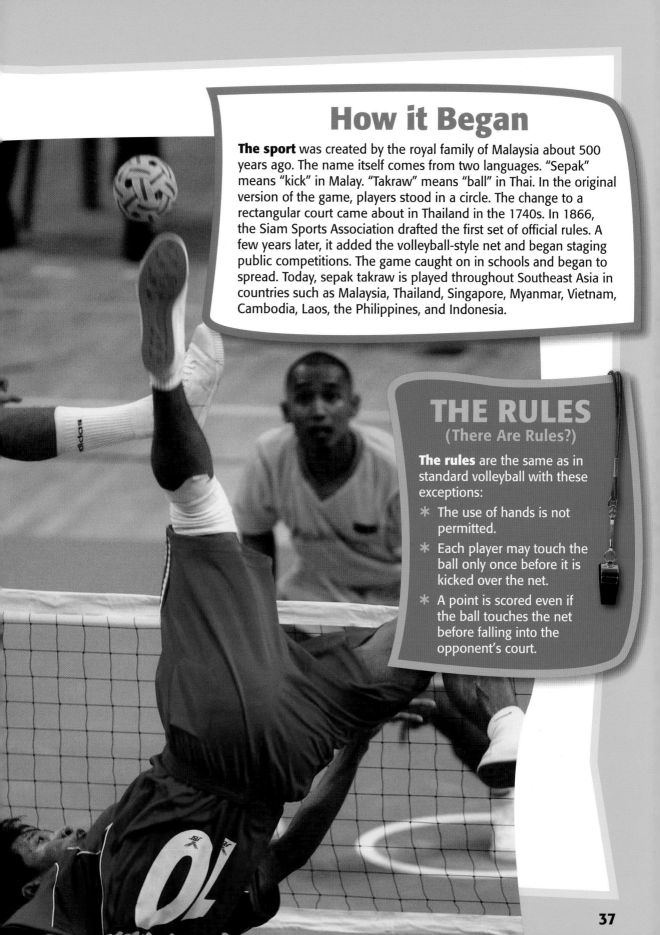

How it Began

The sport was created by the royal family of Malaysia about 500 years ago. The name itself comes from two languages. "Sepak" means "kick" in Malay. "Takraw" means "ball" in Thai. In the original version of the game, players stood in a circle. The change to a rectangular court came about in Thailand in the 1740s. In 1866, the Siam Sports Association drafted the first set of official rules. A few years later, it added the volleyball-style net and began staging public competitions. The game caught on in schools and began to spread. Today, sepak takraw is played throughout Southeast Asia in countries such as Malaysia, Thailand, Singapore, Myanmar, Vietnam, Cambodia, Laos, the Philippines, and Indonesia.

THE RULES
(There Are Rules?)

The rules are the same as in standard volleyball with these exceptions:

* The use of hands is not permitted.
* Each player may touch the ball only once before it is kicked over the net.
* A point is scored even if the ball touches the net before falling into the opponent's court.

BARREL RACING

PLAYED IN: **ITALY**

Twice a year in the village of Montepulciano, Italy, watch out for runaway barrels! As part of an annual religious festival, teams of two men roll giant empty wine barrels around a street course in pursuit of a silk banner for a prize. The races have been going on since 1373!

THE RULES
(There Are Rules?)

* Each neighborhood in the city chooses its two barrel-pushers. They wear the colors of their neighborhood (and thick gloves!).
* The men roll the barrel up and down the streets. The trickiest parts are downhill (don't go too fast!), and uphill (man, this barrel just got really heavy!).
* You can't carry the barrel!

GEAR UP!

* **one barrel**
* **two barrel rollers**

WIFE-CARRYING

This sport was first introduced in Finland and is now also popular in Estonia. Here's how it works: Male competitors race while carrying a female teammate. The object is for the male to carry the female (for a married man, his wife) through a special obstacle course in the fastest time.

THE RULES
(There Are Rules?)

* The official length of the track is 253.5 meters (277 yards).
* The track contains two dry obstacles and one water obstacle.
* All wives who participate must be over 17 years old.
* A wife may weigh no less than 49 kilograms (108 lbs).
* The winner is the couple who completes the course in the shortest time.

GEAR UP!

* 1 man
* 1 woman

CHEESE ROLLING

PLAYED IN: ENGLAND

The central question in cheese rolling is this: Are you faster than a wheel of cheese? This sport from Gloucestershire (where they make cheese, of course!) is pretty simple. From the top of a very steep hill, a round wheel (a large disk) of double Gloucester cheese is released. Competitors then chase the cheese down the hill, usually falling and rolling themselves. The goal is to catch the cheese before it reaches the bottom of the hill. This is one time when playing with your food is encouraged!

Great Moments

* **1826:** cheese rolling is first written about, most likely as a pagan harvest ritual.
* **1941-1954:** a wooden "cheese" is used, due to rationing during and right after World War II.
* **1997:** a record 33 people are injured and the event is cancelled the following year.

The Cheese

KABADDI

PLAYED IN: **INDIA, PAKISTAN, AND SOME SOUTHEAST ASIAN COUNTRIES**

Kabaddi is a unique combination of tag and breath holding. Really. Each team takes turns sending one player, called a "raider," into the other team's territory. His or her job is to tag as many opponents as possible. Here's the catch: The raiders must return to their own side of the court on only one breath. To prove that they are not breathing while chasing their opponents, the invading players must chant the word *kabaddi*. This is a Hindi word meaning "holding of breath." They chant over and over without pausing to breathe. Today, more than 30 countries around the world compete in international tournaments.

THE RULES
(There Are Rules?)

When a raider tags a member of the opposing team, the raider's team gets one point. That team gets a two-point bonus if every player on the opposing team is tagged during the raider's one breath. The raider's turn is over if the raider breathes before returning to his or her side of the court, or if the raider goes out of bounds.

41

CHESS BOXING

PLAYED IN:
EASTERN EUROPE

You circle your opponent in the ring, looking for an opening to connect with a right hook. The bell rings, ending the round. In the next round, you look for an opening so you can capture your opponent's king. Welcome to the world of chess boxing, the weird sport that combines brains and brawn.

PRO TIP

"There is a lot of similarity. Boxing is like a chess match. You're always trying to set up your opponent. The toughest part is coming out of the ring and trying to figure out what was the next move you were planning to make on the chess board. You always plan four or five moves ahead."

—DAVID DEPTO, THE TOP-RATED CHESS BOXER IN THE UNITED STATES

THE RULES
(There Are Rules?)

The sport is a combination of boxing and chess, with the different games alternating after each round. The match begins with a four-minute round of chess, followed by a three-minute round of boxing. There is a one-minute break between rounds. The athletes then alternate rounds until there is a knockout in boxing or a checkmate in chess. If there is no winner, judges decide who wins.

PARKOUR

This sport, also known as freerunning, consists of moving as quickly and smoothly as possible over obstacles such as fences, walls, rocks, buildings, tree branches, or anything else that might block your path. It combines gymnastics, dance, geometry, and guts. Free runners spend as much time trying to do things gracefully as quickly. Some call it an art as much as a sport.

THE RULES
(There Are Rules?)

The goal of parkour is to get from one place to another using only the strength of the human body and objects that are already in place. Typical movements include running, jumping, vaulting, climbing, and balancing.

WORLD ESKIMO-

ALASKAN HIGH KICK

The athlete sits on the floor below a target with one hand holding his or her opposite foot. With the free hand planted on the floor the whole time, the athlete springs up and attempts to kick the target above his head with the free foot.

Every year in Alaska, Inuit Eskimos hold their own Olympics. The sports they play, while they may seem unusual to us, are all based on their cultural heritage and on Arctic survival skills. Carrying, pulling, jumping, and balancing were skills needed to survive though the long Arctic winter. They've been adapted into the sports of the World Eskimo-Indian Olympics. Let's take a look at some of these amazing Alaskan athletes!

DROP THE BOMB

In this test of strength, each contestant is carried in an "iron cross" position by three "spotters." One spotter holds the feet holding both ankles, while the other two each hold one wrist, all while walking. When the person's body or arms begin to sag, the contestant is said to have "dropped the bomb." Whoever goes the farthest before bombing is the winner.

INDIAN OLYMPICS

ONE-FOOT KICK

This high-kick event requires the athlete to jump off the floor using both feet, kick a suspended object with one foot, and then land on the floor on the kicking foot. Jumpers have been known to jump as high as a basketball net.

TWO-FOOT KICK

This event is similar to the one-foot high kick, except here the athlete jumps off the floor using both feet, hits the suspended target with both feet together, and lands with both feet touching the floor at the same time.

SEAL HOP

Balancing only on knuckles and toes, the athlete hops across the gym floor. The event mimics the movement of a seal across the ice. Without flippers, though, the hopper goes as long as his knuckles can stand the pain.

FOUR-MAN CARRY

This cool event mirrors the strength and endurance a native Alaskan needed to carry home a large animal after a hunt. Today, the four-man carry is a distance race in which one contestant carries four men holding onto his body. The farthest carry wins.

EAR-WEIGHT CARRY

Sixteen 1-pound (.45 kg) weights threaded on twine are used in this event. Contestants loop the twine around one ear, stand up, and walk as far as they can. Winning distances of more than 2,000 feet (610 m) are common—as are very sore ears. Ouch!

NALUKATAQ

One person sits on a blanket, or in the more traditional version, a bunch of walrus skins sewn together. The edges of the blanket are grabbed by a large group of people, who toss the person on the blanket high into the air. To pick a winner, the judges look at balance, height, and movements in the air, such as dancing, running in place, spinning, or doing somersaults.

INDEX

PHOTO CREDITS

Adam Lau: 8; AP/Wide World: 4, 5, 11 top, 18, 29, 30 top, 35, 37, 39, 47; Corbis: 11, 27 bottom, 33, 38, 40, 41; dreamstime.com/Steve Allen: 4; dreamstime.com/Julia Barlachenko: 30 bottom; dreamstime.com/designpicssub: 14; dreamstime.com/monkeybusinessimages: 12; dreamstime.com/Paparico: 27 top; Kris Holm: 15; iStock/Stephen Finn: 26; iStock/Joe Michl: 24; iStock/inababes: 32; iStock/Arturoli: 43; Johnson Creek Fire & EMS, Wisconsin/Lloyd Schultz: 21; Mike King: 22, 23; Ronn Murray: 44-46 (all); Press-Register: 10 bottom, 10-11 main; Speed Golf Association: 31

ABOUT THE AUTHOR

MICHAEL TEITELBAUM has never tossed a mullet, ironed a shirt on a tightrope, or raced against cheese. However, he has been a writer and editor of children's books and magazines for more than 20 years. He was editor of *Little League Magazine For Kids*, and *Spider-Man Magazine* for Marvel Comics. Michael's most recent nonfiction includes *Jackie Robinson: Champion For Equality*. Michael's fiction includes *The Scary States of America* and *Backyard Sports,* as well as books based on characters ranging from Spider-Man and Batman to Garfield and Kermit the Frog. Michael and his wife, Sheleigah, live in a 170-year old farmhouse in the Catskill Mountains of upstate New York.